The CONSTITUTION

A Heavenly Banner

The CONSTITUTION

A Heavenly Banner

Ezra Taft Benson

DESERET
BOOK

SALT LAKE CITY, UTAH

Cover photo of Constitution © Comstock Images
Cover photo of flag © Getty Images

© 1986 Deseret Book Company

DESERET BOOK is a registered trademark of Deseret Book Company.

Visit us at DeseretBook.com

ISBN 978-0-87579-067-1

Printed in the United States of America
Worzalla Publishing Co., Stevens Point, WI

10   9   8   7   6   5   4   3   2   1

$\mathcal{M}$y fellow Americans, on the 17th day of September, 1987, we commemorate the two-hundredth birthday of the Constitutional Convention, which gave birth to the document that Gladstone said is "the most wonderful work ever struck off at a given time by the brain and purpose of man."

I heartily endorse this assessment. It would be erroneous for us, however, to conclude that the document was the sole genius of the Founding Fathers. Theirs was a combined wisdom derived from heavenly inspiration, knowledge of political government from ages past, and the crucible of their own experience.

We pay honor—honor to the document itself, honor to the men who framed it, and honor to the God who inspired it and made possible its coming forth.

SOME BASIC PRINCIPLES

To understand the significance of the Constitution, we must first understand some basic, eternal principles. These principles have their beginning in the premortal councils of heaven.

The Principle of Agency

The first basic principle is agency. We understand that the purpose of the council in heaven was to announce and present the plan of redemption for the salvation of all of God's children. The council was called so that every man and woman could sustain the provisions of the Father's plan, which required that all people obtain mortal bodies, be tried and proven in all things, and have opportunity to choose of their own free will to obey the laws and ordinances essential to their exaltation.

Because a fallen condition was an essential part of this plan, an infinite, eternal sacrifice was also required to redeem us from this state. We are all familiar with the facts: how Lucifer—a personage of prominence—sought to amend the plan, while Jehovah sustained the plan. The Prophet Joseph Smith explained how this difference led to the war in heaven: "The contention in heaven was—Jesus said there would be certain souls that would not be saved; and the devil said he could save them all, and laid his plans before the grand council, who gave their vote in favor of Jesus Christ. So the devil rose up in rebellion against God, and was cast down."

The central issue in that council, then, was: Shall the children of God have untrammeled agency to choose the course they should follow, whether good or evil, or shall they be coerced and forced to be obedient? Christ and all who followed Him stood for the former proposition—freedom of choice; Satan stood for the latter—coercion and force. Because Satan and those who stood with him would not accept the vote of the council, but rose up in rebellion, they were cast down to the earth, where they have continued to foster the same plan. The war that began in heaven is not yet over. The conflict continues on the battlefield of mortality. And one of Lucifer's primary strategies has been to restrict our agency through the power of earthly governments. Proof of this is found in the long history of humanity.

When the first worldly government began as a theocracy, Adam's descendants soon departed from this perfect order and degenerated into various political systems. The result has been human misery and, for most of humankind, subjugation to some despotic government.

Look back in retrospect on almost six thousand years of human history! Freedom's moments have been infrequent and exceptional. From Nimrod to Napoleon, the conventional political ideology has been that the rights of life, liberty, and property were subject to a sovereign's will, rather than God-given. We must appreciate that we live in one of history's most exceptional moments—in a nation and a time of unprecedented freedom. Freedom as we know it has been experienced by perhaps less than one percent of the human family.

The Proper Role of Government

The second basic principle concerns the function and proper role of government. I should like to outline in clear, concise, and straightforward terms the guidelines that determine, now and in the future, my attitudes and actions toward all domestic proposals and projects of government. These are the principles that, in my opinion, proclaim the proper role of government in the domestic affairs of the nation:

[I] believe that governments were instituted of God for the benefit of man; and that he holds men accountable for their acts in relation to them.

[I] believe that no government can exist in peace, except such laws are framed and held inviolate as will secure to each individual the free exercise of conscience, the right and control of property, and the protection of life. . . .

[I] believe that all men are bound to sustain and uphold the respective governments in which they reside, while protected in their inherent and inalienable rights by the laws of such governments. (D&C 134:1–2, 5.)

In other words, the most important single function of government is to secure the rights and freedoms of individual citizens.

The Source of Human Rights

The third important principle pertains to the source of basic human rights. Thomas Paine, back in the days of the American Revolution, explained: "Rights are not gifts from one man to another, nor from one class of men to another. . . . It is impossible to discover any origin of rights otherwise than in the origin of man; it consequently follows that rights appertain to man in right of his existence, and must therefore be equal to every man."

The great Thomas Jefferson asked: "Can the liberties of a nation be thought secure when we have removed their only firm basis, a conviction in the minds of the people that these liberties are of the gift of God? That they are not to be violated but with his wrath?"

The feelings of these great men are in keeping with the revelations of God through His prophet, who said: "Men are free according to the flesh . . . and they are free to choose liberty and eternal life . . . or to choose captivity and death." (2 Nephi 2:27.)

Rights are either *God-given* as part of the divine plan, or they are *granted by government* as part of the political plan. Reason, necessity, tradition, and religious conviction all lead me to accept the divine origin of these rights. If we accept the premise that human rights are granted by government, then we must be willing to accept the corollary that they can be denied by government. I, for one, shall never accept that premise. As the French political economist Frederic Bastiat phrased it so succinctly, "Life, liberty, and property do not exist because men have made laws. On the contrary, it was the fact that life, liberty, and property existed beforehand that caused men to make laws in the first place."

We must ever keep in mind the inspired words of Thomas Jefferson, as found in the Declaration of Independence: "We hold these truths to be self-evident, that all men are created equal, that they are endowed by their Creator with certain unalienable Rights, that among these are Life, Liberty and the pursuit of Happiness. That to secure these rights, Governments are instituted among Men, deriving their just powers from the consent of the governed."

People Are Superior to Governments

The fourth basic principle we must understand is that people are superior to the governments they form. Since God created people with certain inalienable rights, and they, in turn, created government to help secure and safeguard those rights, it follows that the people are superior to the creature they created. We are superior to government and should remain master over it, not the other way around. Government is nothing more nor less than a relatively small group of citizens who have been hired, in a sense, by the rest of us to perform certain functions and discharge certain responsibilities we have authorized. It stands to reason that the government itself has no innate power nor privilege to do anything. Its only source of authority and power is from the people who have created it. This is made clear in the Preamble of the Constitution of the United States, which reads: "WE THE PEOPLE . . . do ordain and establish this Constitution for the United States of America."

Governments Should Have Limited Powers

The final principle that is basic to our understanding of the Constitution is that governments should have only limited powers. The important thing to keep in mind is that the people who have created their government can give to that government only such powers as they, themselves, have in the first place. Obviously, they cannot give that which they do not possess. So the question boils down to this: What powers properly belong to each and every person in the absence of and prior to the establishment of any organized form of government?

In a primitive state, there is no doubt that every individual would be justified in using force, if necessary, for defense against physical harm, against theft of the fruits of his labor, and against enslavement by another.

Indeed, the early pioneers found that a great deal of their time and energy was spent defending all three—defending themselves, their property, and their liberty—in what properly was called the "lawless West." In order for people to prosper, they cannot afford to spend their time constantly guarding family, fields, and property against attack and theft, so they join together with their neighbors and hire a sheriff. At this precise moment, government is born. The individual citizens delegate to the sheriff their unquestionable right to protect themselves. The sheriff now does for them only what they had a right to do for themselves—nothing more. Quoting from Bastiat: "If every person has the right to defend—even by force—his person, his liberty, and his property, then it follows that a group of men have the right to organize and support a common force to protect these rights constantly. Thus the principle of collective right—its reason for existing, its lawfulness—is based on individual right."

The proper function of government, then, is limited to those spheres of activity within which the individual citizen has the right to act. By deriving its just powers from the governed, government becomes primarily a mechanism for defense against bodily harm, theft, and involuntary servitude. It cannot claim the power to redistribute money or property nor to force reluctant citizens to perform acts of charity against their will. Government is created by the people. No individual possesses the power to take another's wealth or to force others to do good, so no government has the right to do such things either. The creature cannot exceed the creator.

My attitude toward government is succinctly expressed by the following provision taken from the Alabama Constitution: "The sole object and only legitimate end of government is to protect the citizen in the enjoyment of life, liberty, and property, and when the government assumes other functions it is usurpation and oppression." (Article 1, Section 35.)

THE CONSTITUTION AND ITS COMING FORTH

With these basic principles firmly in mind, let us now turn to a discussion of the inspired document we call the Constitution. My purpose is not to recite the events that led to the American Revolution—we are all familiar with these. But I would say this: History is not an accident. Events are foreknown to God. His superintending influence is behind the actions of His righteous children. Long before America was even discovered, the Lord was moving and shaping events that would lead to the coming forth of the remarkable form of government established by the Constitution. America had to be free and independent to fulfill this destiny. I commend to you as excellent reading on this subject Elder Mark E. Petersen's book *The Great Prologue* (Salt Lake City: Deseret Book Co., 1975). As expressed so eloquently by John Adams before the signing of the Declaration, "There's a divinity that shapes our ends." Though mortal eyes and minds cannot fathom the end from the beginning, God does.

Every true American and true friend of liberty should love our inspired Constitution. Its creation was a miracle. In a letter to Marquis de LaFayette, on February 7, 1788, George Washington stated: "It appears to me . . . little short of a miracle, that the Delegates from so many different states (which States you know are also different from each other, in their manners, circumstances, and prejudices) should unite in forming a system of national Government, so little liable to well founded objections."

GOD RAISED UP WISE MEN TO CREATE THE CONSTITUTION

George Washington referred to this document as a miracle. This miracle could only have been performed by exceptional men. In a revelation to the Prophet Joseph Smith, the Savior declared, "I established the Constitution of this land, by the hands of wise men whom I raised up unto this very purpose." (D&C 101:80.) These were not ordinary men, but men chosen and held in reserve by the Lord for this very purpose.

Shortly after President Spencer W. Kimball became president of the Church, we met together in one of our weekly meetings. We spoke of the sacred records that are in the vaults of the various temples in the Church. As I was to fill a conference assignment at St. George, President Kimball asked me to go into the vault and check the early records. As I did so, I realized the fulfillment of a dream I had had ever since learning of the visit of the Founding Fathers to the St. George Temple. I saw with my own eyes the records of the work that was done for the Founding Fathers of this great nation, beginning with George Washington. Think of it, the Founding Fathers of this nation, those great men, appeared within those sacred walls and had their vicarious work done for them.

Wilford Woodruff's Testimony

President Wilford Woodruff spoke of this experience in these words: "Before I left St. George, the spirits of the dead gathered around me, wanting to know why we did not redeem them. Said they, 'You have had the use of the Endowment House for a number of years, and yet nothing has ever been done for us. We laid the foundation of the government you now enjoy, and we never apostatized from it, but we remained true to it and were faithful to God.' These were the signers of the Declaration of Independence, and they waited on me for two days and two nights. . . . I straightway went into the baptismal font and called upon Brother McCallister to baptize me for the signers of the Declaration of Independence, and fifty other eminent men, making one hundred in all, including John Wesley, Columbus, and others."

President Woodruff was an apostle and the president of the St. George Temple at the time of the appearing of these great men. These noble spirits came there with divine permission—evidence that this work of salvation goes forward on both sides of the veil.

At a later conference, in April 1898, after he became president of the Church, President Woodruff declared that "those men who laid the foundation of this American government and signed the Declaration of Independence were the best spirits the God of heaven could find on the face of the earth. They were choice spirits . . . [and] were inspired of the Lord." We honor those men today. We are the grateful beneficiaries of their noble work.

The Constitution, an Inspired Document

During an address before members of the Church in 1855, President Brigham Young said: "The . . .

Constitution of our country . . . was dictated by the invisible operations of the Almighty. . . . God's purposes, in raising up these men and inspiring them with daring sufficient to surmount every opposing power, was to prepare the way for the formation of a true republican government. . . .

"It was the voice of the Lord inspiring all those worthy men who bore influence in those trying times, not only to go forth in battle, but to exercise wisdom in council, fortitude, courage, and endurance in the tested field, as well as subsequently to form and adopt those wise and efficient measures which secured to themselves and succeeding generations, the blessing of a free and independent government."

Pure Motives of the Founding Fathers

James Madison, referred to as the Father of the Constitution, wrote a fitting tribute about his renowned colleagues: "Whatever may be the judgment pronounced on the competency of the architects of the Constitution, or whatever may be the destiny of the edifice prepared by them, I feel it a duty to express my profound and solemn conviction, derived from my intimate opportunity of observing and appreciating the views of the Convention, collectively and individually, that there never was an assembly of men, charged with a great and arduous trust, who were more pure in their motives, or more exclusively or anxiously devoted to the object committed to them, than were the members of the Federal Convention of 1787."

THE LORD APPROVED THE CONSTITUTION

But we honor more than those who brought forth the Constitution. We honor the Lord who revealed it. God Himself has borne witness to the fact that He is pleased with the final product of the work of these great patriots.

In a revelation to the Prophet Joseph Smith on August 6, 1833, the Savior admonished: "I, the Lord, justify you, and your brethren of my church, in befriending that law which is the constitutional law of the land." (D&C 98:6.)

In the Kirtland Temple dedicatory prayer, given on March 27, 1836, the Lord directed the Prophet Joseph to say: "May those principles, which were so honorably and nobly defended, namely, the Constitution of our land, by our fathers, be established forever." (D&C 109:54.)

A few years later, Joseph Smith, while unjustly incarcerated in a cold and depressing cell of Liberty Jail at Clay County, Missouri, frequently bore his testimony of the document's divinity: "The Constitution of the United States is a glorious standard; and is founded in the wisdom of God. It is a heavenly banner."

The coming forth of the Constitution is of such transcendent importance in the Lord's plan that ancient prophets foresaw this event and prophesied of it. In the dedicatory prayer for the Idaho Falls Temple, President George Albert Smith indicated that the Constitution fulfilled the ancient prophecy of Isaiah that "out of Zion shall go forth the law." (Isaiah 2:3.)

He said: "We thank thee that thou hast revealed to us that those who gave us our constitutional form of government were wise men in thy sight and that thou didst raise them up for the very purpose of putting forth that sacred document [the Constitution of the United States]. . . .

"We pray that kings and rulers and the people of all nations under heaven may be persuaded of the blessings enjoyed by the people of this land by reason of their freedom and under thy guidance and be constrained to adopt similar governmental systems, thus to fulfill the ancient prophecy of Isaiah and Micah that 'out of Zion shall go forth the law, and the word of the Lord from Jerusalem.'" (*Improvement Era*, October 1945, p. 564.)

In the final analysis, what the framers did, under the inspiration of God, was to draft a document that merited the approval of God Himself, who declared that it should "be maintained for the rights and protection of all flesh." (D&C 101:77.) How this was accomplished merits our further consideration.

THE DOCUMENT ITSELF

The Constitution consists of seven separate articles. The first three establish the three branches of our government—the legislative, the executive, and the judicial. The fourth article describes matters pertaining to states, most significantly the guarantee of a republican form of government to every state of the Union. Article 5 defines the amendment procedure of the document, a deliberately difficult process that should be clearly understood by every citizen. Article 6 covers several miscellaneous items, including a definition of the supreme law of the land, namely, the Constitution itself, the laws of the United States, and all treaties made. Article 7, the last, explains how the Constitution is to be ratified.

After ratification of the document, ten amendments were added and designated as our Bill of

Rights. To date, the Constitution has been amended twenty-six times, the most recent amendment giving young people the right to vote at age eighteen.

Now to look at some of the major provisions of the document itself. Many principles could be examined, but I mention five as being crucial to the preservation of our freedom. If we understand the workability of these, we have taken the first step in defending our freedoms.

MAJOR PROVISIONS OF THE DOCUMENT

The major provisions of the Constitution are as follows:

Sovereignty of the People

First: Sovereignty lies in the people themselves. Every governmental system has a sovereign, one or several who possess all the executive, legislative, and judicial powers. That sovereign may be an individual, a group, or the people themselves. Broadly speaking, there are only two governmental systems in the world today. One system recognizes that the sovereign power is vested in one person or a group of people who serve as head of state. This kind of government rests on the premise that the ruler grants to the people the rights and powers the ruler thinks they should have. This system is wrong, regardless of how benevolent the dictator may be, because it denies that which belongs to all people inalienably—the right of life, liberty, and property.

The Founding Fathers believed in common law, which holds that true sovereignty rests with the people. Believing this to be in accord with truth, they inserted this imperative in the Declaration of Independence: "To secure these rights [life, liberty, and the pursuit of happiness], governments are instituted among men, deriving their just powers from the consent of the governed."

Separation of Powers

Second: To safeguard these rights, the Founding Fathers provided for the separation of powers among the three branches of government—the legislative, the executive, and the judicial. Each was to be independent of the other, yet each was to work in a unified relationship. As the great constitutionalist President J. Reuben Clark noted: "It is the union of independence and dependence of these branches—legislative, executive, and judicial—and of the governmental functions possessed by each of them, that constitutes the marvelous genius of this unrivaled document. . . . It was here that the divine inspiration came. It was truly a miracle." (*Church News,* November 29, 1952, p. 12.)

In order to avoid a concentration of power in any one branch, the Founding Fathers created a system of government that provided checks and balances. Congress could pass laws, but the president could check these laws with a veto. Congress, however, could override the veto and, by its means of initiative in taxation, could further restrain the executive department. The Supreme Court could nullify laws passed by the Congress and signed by the president, but Congress could limit the court's appellate jurisdiction. The president could appoint judges for their lifetime with the consent of the Senate.

The use of checks and balances was deliberately designed, first, to make it difficult for a minority of the people to control the government, and, second, to place restraint on the government itself.

Limited Powers of Government

Third: The powers the people granted to the three branches of government were specifically limited. Originally, the Constitution permitted few powers to the federal government, these chiefly being, as Thomas Jefferson said, the powers concerning "war, peace, negotiation and distributing to every one exactly the functions he is competent to. Let the national government be entrusted with the defence of the nation, and its foreign and federal relations; the State governments with the *civil rights*, law, police, and administration of what concerns the State generally, the counties with the local concerns of the counties, and each ward direct the interests within itself. It is by dividing and subdividing these republics from the great national one down through all its subordinations . . . that all will be done for the best. *What has destroyed liberty and the rights of man in every government which has ever existed under the sun? The generalizing and concentrating all cares and powers into one body."*

The Founding Fathers well understood human nature and its tendency to exercise unrighteous dominion when given authority. A Constitution was therefore designed to limit government to certain enumerated functions, beyond which was tyranny.

The Principle of Representation

Fourth: Our Constitutional government is based on the principle of representation. The principle of representation means that we have delegated to an elected official the power to represent us. The Constitution provides for both direct representation and indirect representation. Both forms of representation provide a tempering influence on pure democracy.

The House of Representatives was elected for only two years by direct vote of the people on a population basis. This concession to democracy was balanced by the establishment of a Senate, originally elected for six years, by state legislatures. This was an ingenious system whereby the Senate, not directly responsible to the people, could act as a restraining influence on any demagoguery by the House. No law could be passed without the majority approval of the House, whose members were directly elected by the populace; but also, a law had to have the majority concurrence of the Senate, who at that time were not elected by the people. In this way, the passions and impulses of the majority vote were checked.

The intent was to protect the individual's and the minority's rights to life, liberty, and the fruits of their labors—property. These rights were not to be subject to majority vote.

We all know, of course, that this system was altered by amendment so that today both House and Senate are elected by direct popular vote.

A Moral and Righteous People

Fifth: The Constitution was designed to work only with a moral and righteous people. "Our Constitution," said

John Adams (first vice-president and second president of the United States), "was made only for a moral and religious people. It is wholly inadequate to the government of any other."

In recognizing God as the source of their rights, the Founding Fathers declared Him to be the ultimate authority for their basis of law. This led them to the conviction that people do not make law but merely acknowledge preexisting law, giving it specific application. The Constitution was conceived to be such an expression of high law. And when their work was done, Madison wrote: "It is impossible for the man of pious reflection not to perceive in it a finger of that Almighty hand which has been so frequently and signally extended to our relief in the critical stage of the revolution." (*The Federalist,* no. 37.)

THE CRISIS OF OUR CONSTITUTION

This, then, is the ingenious and inspired document created by these good and wise men for the benefit and blessing of future generations. We are the beneficiaries of their work, and we owe a great debt of gratitude to them and to our God who led them in their task.

In a talk to the youth of the Church concerning America and the Constitution, President J. Reuben Clark said: "May I tell you a few of the elemental principles? It [the Constitution] gave us, for perhaps the first time in all history, a republic with the three basic divisions of government—the Legislative, Executive, and Judicial—mutually and completely independent, the one from the other, under which it is not possible for any branch of government legally to set up a system by which that branch can first conceive what it wants to do, then make the law ordering its doing and then, itself, judge its own enforcement of its own law, a system that has always brought extortion, oppression, intimidation, tyranny, despotism—a system that every dictator has employed and must employ." (*Improvement Era*, July 1940, p. 443.)

It is now two hundred years since the Constitution was written. Have we been wise beneficiaries of the gift entrusted to us? Have we valued and protected the principles laid down by this great document?

At this bicentennial celebration we must, with sadness, say that we have not been wise in keeping the trust of our Founding Fathers. For the past two centuries, those who do not prize freedom have chipped away at every major clause of our Constitution until today we face a crisis of great dimensions.

Erosion of Our Freedoms

Let me cite, just briefly, two examples of the erosion of our constitutional freedoms. Both have come about because we, the people, have allowed the government to ignore one of the most fundamental stipulations of the Constitution—namely, the separation of powers.

In recent years, we have allowed Congress to fund numerous federal agencies. While these agencies may provide some needed services and protection of rights, they also encroach significantly on our constitutional rights. The number of agencies seems to grow continually to regulate and control the lives of millions of citizens.

What many fail to realize is that most of these federal agencies are unconstitutional. Why are they unconstitutional? They are unconstitutional because they concentrate the functions of the legislative, executive, and judicial branches under one head. They have, in other words, power to make rulings, enforce rulings, and adjudicate penalties when rulings are violated. They are unconstitutional because they represent an assumption of power not delegated to the executive branch by the people. They are also unconstitutional because the people have no power to recall administrative agency personnel by their vote.

A second example of this abandonment of fundamental principles can be found in recent trends in the U.S. Supreme Court. Note what Lino A. Graglia, a professor of law at the University of Texas, has to say about this: "Purporting merely to enforce the Constitution, the Supreme Court has for some thirty years usurped and exercised legislative powers that its predecessors could not have dreamed of, making itself the most powerful and important institution of government in regard to the nature and quality of life in our society. . . .

"It has literally decided issues of life and death, removing from the states the power to prevent or significantly restrain the practice of abortion, and, after effectively prohibiting capital punishment for two decades, now imposing such costly and time-consuming restrictions on its use as almost to amount to prohibition.

"In the area of morality and religion, the Court has removed from both the federal and state government nearly all power to prohibit the distribution and sale or exhibition of pornographic materials. . . . It has prohibited the states from providing for prayer or Bible-reading in the public schools.

"The Court has created for criminal defendants rights that do not exist under any other system of law—for example, the possibility of almost endless appeals with all costs paid by the state—and which have made the prosecution and conviction of criminals so complex and difficult as to make the attempt frequently seem not worthwhile. It has severely restricted the power of the states and cities to limit marches and other public demonstrations and otherwise maintain order in the streets and other public places."

To all who have discerning eyes, it is apparent that the republican form of government established by our noble forefathers cannot long endure once fundamental principles are abandoned. Momentum is gathering for another conflict—a repetition of the crisis of two hundred years ago. This collision of ideas is worldwide. Another monumental moment is soon to be born. The issue is the same that precipitated the great premortal conflict—will men be free to determine their own course of action or must they be coerced?

The Prophecy of Joseph Smith

We are fast approaching that moment prophesied by Joseph Smith when he said: "Even this nation will be on the very verge of crumbling to pieces and tumbling to the ground, and when the Constitution is upon the brink of ruin, this people will be the staff upon which the nation shall lean, and they shall bear the Constitution away from the very verge of destruction." (July 19, 1840, Church Historian's Office, Salt Lake City.)

The Need to Prepare

Will we be prepared? Will we be among those who will "bear the Constitution away from the very verge of destruction?" If we desire to be numbered among those who will, here are some things we must do:

1. *We must be righteous and moral.* We must live the gospel principles—all of them. We have no right to expect a higher degree of morality from those who represent us than what we ourselves are. In the final analysis, people generally get the kind of government they deserve. To live a higher law means we will not seek to receive what we have not earned by our own labor. It means we will remember that government owes us nothing. It means we will keep the laws of the land. It means we will look to God as our Lawgiver and the Source of our liberty.

2. *We must learn the principles of the Constitution and then abide by its precepts.* We have been instructed again and again to reflect more intently on the meaning and importance of the Constitution and to adhere to

its principles. What have we done about this instruction? Have we read the Constitution and pondered it? Are we aware of its principles? Could we defend it? Can we recognize when a law is constitutionally unsound? The Church will not tell us how to do this, but we are admonished to do it. I quote Abraham Lincoln: "Let [the Constitution] be taught in schools, in seminaries, and in colleges, let it be written in primers, in spelling books and in almanacs, let it be preached from the pulpit, proclaimed in legislative halls, and enforced in courts of justice. And, in short, let it become the political religion of the nation."

3. *We must become involved in civic affairs.* As citizens of this republic, we cannot do our duty and be idle spectators. It is vital that we follow this counsel from the Lord: "I, the Lord God, make you free, therefore ye are free indeed; and the law also maketh you free. Nevertheless, when the wicked rule the people mourn. Wherefore, honest men and wise men should be sought for diligently, and good men and wise men ye should observe to uphold; otherwise whatsoever is less than these cometh of evil. And I give unto you a commandment, that ye shall forsake all evil and cleave unto all good, that ye shall live by every word which proceedeth forth out of the mouth of God." (D&C 98:8–11.)

Note the qualities that the Lord demands in those who are to represent us. They must be good, wise, and honest. Some leaders may be honest and good but unwise in legislation they choose to support. Others may possess wisdom but be dishonest and unvirtuous. We must be concerted in our desires and efforts to see men and women represent us who possess all three of these qualities.

4. *We must make our influence felt by our vote, our letters, and our advice.* We must be wisely informed and let others know how we feel. We must take part in local precinct meetings and select delegates who will truly represent our feelings.

I have faith that the Constitution will be saved as prophesied by Joseph Smith. But it will not be saved in Washington. It will be saved by the citizens of this nation who love and cherish freedom. It will be saved by enlightened members of this Church—men and women who will subscribe to and abide by the principles of the Constitution.

THE CONSTITUTION REQUIRES OUR LOYALTY AND SUPPORT

I reverence the Constitution of the United States as a sacred document. To me its words are akin to the revelations of God, for God has placed His stamp of approval on the Constitution of this land. I testify that the God of heaven sent some of His choicest spirits to lay the foundation of this government, and He has sent other choice spirits—even you who read my words—to preserve it.

Our feelings for this marvelous document should be the same as those attributed to John Adams by Daniel Webster. When others were vacillating on whether to adopt the Declaration of Independence, the sentiments of John Adams were these: "Sink or swim, live or die, survive or perish, I give my hand and my heart to this vote. It is true, indeed, that in the beginning we aimed not at independence. But there's a Divinity that shapes our ends. . . . Why, then, should we defer the Declaration? . . . You and I, indeed, may rue it. We may not live to see the time when this Declaration shall be made good. We may die; die Colonists, die slaves, die, it may be, ignominiously and on the scaffold.

"Be it so. Be it so.

"If it be the pleasure of Heaven that my country shall require the poor offering of my life, the victim shall be ready. . . . But while I do live, let me have a country, or at least the hope of a country, and that a free country.

"But whatever may be our fate, be assured . . . that this Declaration will stand. It may cost treasure, and it may cost blood, but it will stand and it will richly compensate for both.

"Through the thick gloom of the present, I see the brightness of the future as the sun in heaven. We shall make this a glorious, an immortal day. When we are in our graves, our children will honor it. They will celebrate it with thanksgiving, with festivity, with bonfires, and illuminations. . . .

"Before God, I believe the hour is come. My judgment approves this measure, and my whole heart is in it. All that I have, and all that I am, and all that I hope, in this life, I am now ready here to stake upon it; and I leave off as I began, that live or die, survive or perish, I am for the Declaration. It is my living sentiment, and by the blessing of God it shall be my dying sentiment. Independence now, and Independence forever."

We, the blessed beneficiaries, likewise face difficult days in this beloved land, "a land which is choice above all other lands." (Ether 2:10.)

It may also cost us blood before we are through. It is my conviction, however, that when the Lord comes, the Stars and Stripes will be floating on the breeze over this people. May it be so, and may God give us the faith and the courage exhibited by those patriots who pledged their lives and fortunes that we might be free.

BIBLIOGRAPHY

Bastiat, Frederic. *The Law.* Translated by Dean Russell. Irvington-on-Hudson, New York: The Foundation for Economic Education, 1950.

Gladstone, William E. *Gleanings of Past Years,* 1843–78, 7 vols. London: John Murray, 1879.

Howe, John R., Jr. *The Changing Political Thought of John Adams.* Princeton, New Jersey: Princeton University Press, 1966.

Jefferson, Thomas. *The Writings of Thomas Jefferson.* Edited by Albert E. Bergh. 20 vols. Washington, D.C.: Thomas Jefferson Memorial Association, 1907.

Lincoln, Abraham. *Complete Works of Abraham Lincoln.* Edited by John G. Nicolay and John Hay. 12 vols. New York: Francis D. Tandy Company, 1905.

Paine, Thomas. *The Political Writings of Thomas Paine.* 2 vols. Boston: J. P. Mendum, Investigator Office, 1870.

Smith, Joseph. *History of The Church of Jesus Christ of Latter-day Saints.* 7 vols. 2d ed. rev. Edited by B. H. Roberts. Salt Lake City: The Church of Jesus Christ of Latter-day Saints, 1932–51.

———. *Teachings of the Prophet Joseph Smith.* Selected by Joseph Fielding Smith. Salt Lake City: Deseret Book Company, 1938.

Washington, George. *The Writings of George Washington.* Edited by John D. Fitzpatrick. Washington, D.C.: United States Printing Office, 1931–44.

Webster, Daniel. *The Works of Daniel Webster.* 6 vols. 4th ed. Boston: Charles C. Little and James Brown, 1951.

Whitney, David C., ed. *Founders of Freedom in America.* Chicago: J. G. Ferguson Publishing Company, 1965.

Woodruff, Wilford. *Discourses of Wilford Woodruff.* Selected by G. Homer Durham. Salt Lake City: Bookcraft, 1946.

Young, Brigham. *Discourses of Brigham Young.* Selected and arranged by John A. Widtsoe. Salt Lake City: Deseret Book Company, 1954.